FAKE NEWS

How Satan's Lies Are Deceiving Millions

D1004821

How Satan's Lies Are Deceiving Millions

JIM GILLEY

Pacific Press®
Publishing Association
Nampa, Idaho | Oshawa, Ontario, Canada
www.pacificpress.com

Cover design by Gerald Lee Monks
Cover design resources from iStockphoto/rzarek; iStockphoto
   /A-Digit
Inside design by Aaron Troia

Additional copies of this book are available to purchase by
calling toll-free 1-800-765-6955 or by visiting http://www
.adventistbookcenter.com.

ISBN: 978-0-8163-6456-5

July 2018

Dedication

To Don Jacobsen—my teacher, mentor, and loyal friend.

Contents

CHAPTER 1

Fake News Is Nothing New!

We hear a lot of talk today about *fake news*. When I was growing up, people trusted newspapers and the commentators on TV and radio news broadcasts. There were only three major TV networks back then, and we believed the things we heard on the nightly news. Today we have access to many cable new outlets broadcasting 24/7, and they all seem to have a slant on the news—right, left, conservative, or liberal—so that you can listen to the news program that agrees with your own view of things. Mainstream media and cable news outlets are equally to blame for all the confusion, quoting unnamed sources and putting out stories that agree with their point of view.

News programs have become creative, not only reporting what's happening but also endlessly discussing and commenting on it. For many, the news has become more about entertainment than about information. No wonder we hear accusations of *fake news* being hurled left and right.

And it's not just cable TV programs. The internet is a source that can be partially or entirely false. Social media provides outlets for anyone to post almost anything, making it very difficult to know what's true and what isn't. Opinion disguised as fact, disinformation, and outright lies abound on the internet. As a result, elections are affected, reputations are ruined, and world leaders are embarrassed or are even sometimes forced to resign. Much of what is on the internet and social media sites can't be relied on. It is *fake news*!

Pure truth is hard to come by, not only in the news but in the world of business. We've all learned to take the claims of TV commercials with a grain of salt. That product can't *really* be the most beautiful, economical, fastest-acting, newest, and best sleep ever!

Yes, *fake news* is a hot topic right now. In fact, it's such a hot topic that we sometimes think it has just burst on the scene. The reality is that *fake news* is nothing new. It has been around for a long time—a very long time. It actually started before this world ever existed. *Fake news* began in a most unusual place: it started in heaven.

Heaven?

"But," someone says, "I thought everything was pure and true and holy and perfect in heaven. How could there be *fake news* in heaven?"

Heaven became tainted with *fake news* when a perfect, holy created being named Lucifer decided he should take God's place! Here's how the Bible describes what happened: "How you are fallen from heaven, O Lucifer, son of the morning! . . . For you have said in your heart: . . . 'I will exalt my throne above the stars of God; . . . I will be like the Most High' " (Isaiah 14:12–14).

God created Lucifer as a perfect, beautiful angel, but Lucifer wanted more. He wanted to be "like the Most High." Of course, we all should want to be like God in our characters. But Lucifer didn't just want to be *like* God; he wanted to *be* God. He wanted to push God off His throne, take over heaven, and become the ruler of the universe.

So Lucifer rebelled against God in heaven. He began by starting a *fake-news* campaign about God among the angels. We don't know exactly what his accusations were, but they may have gone something like this: "Do you think God really has our best interests at heart? We shouldn't have to be restricted by God's rules and laws; after all, we angels are perfect! Don't you think God is too strict?" And this continued on and on until the angels became confused. After this *fake news*, some of them began to think that Lucifer was right and that God was not treating them fairly. In fact, Lucifer's campaign of *fake news* was so successful that about a third of the angels eventually joined his rebellion against God (Revelation 12:4).

Lucifer continued fanning the flames of his fake-news campaign until heaven broke out in open rebellion and warfare. It appears that he and the angels who joined him actually tried to take God's kingdom by force! War erupted in heaven itself—the very first war.

God's Word describes what happened in this conflict: "Michael [Christ] and his angels fought with the dragon [Lucifer]; and the dragon and his angels fought, but they did not prevail, nor was a place found for them in heaven any longer. So the great dragon was cast out, that serpent of old, called the Devil and Satan, who deceives the whole world; he was cast to the earth, and his angels were cast out with him" (Revelation 12:7–9). War and conflict—those were the end results of the campaign of *fake news* Lucifer started in heaven itself.

Did you notice where Lucifer ended up when he lost the war in heaven and was cast out? He and his angels were cast down to our earth. And did you notice how the Bible describes him? It calls him "Satan," the one "who deceives the whole world." Deception. *Fake news.* That is the devil's signature characteristic. Wherever you find the devil, you will find deception and conflict.

If he is in your home, there will be conflict. If he is in your heart, there will be conflict. You may even find the devil in your church, and if so, there will be deception and conflict in your church. In fact, the devil works harder in churches than he does anywhere else. He's not worried about bars and casinos and nightclubs. He already controls them. If he can come into the church and deceive people and sow conflict and confusion, he will be all the more successful. That is why there is *fake news* today even in the church. In the Old Testament, Satan led God's people into idol worship and apostasy over and over again. He didn't try to get them to reject God and religion completely. Instead, he spread *fake news* and deceived them into false worship and false ideas about God. He's still doing the same today.

There is *fake news* in many churches today. Why do different churches teach different doctrines that don't agree with each other? It is because Satan is continuing the same old *fake-news* campaign he began so long ago in heaven. He is sowing confusion about who God is, what He is like, and what truth is.

But in the midst of the confusion and deception that Satan is trying to bring into religion and into people's minds, there is one place we can find the pure, unadulterated truth—the Bible, God's holy Word. The Bible says that God's holy word is like "a light that shines in a dark place" and that we should pay attention to it (2 Peter 1:19). It says that in God's Word, the Bible, we find the truth; it is our source of what is true about God and His will for our lives (John 17:17). "The word of the LORD endures forever" (1 Peter 1:25).

Satan has twisted God's truth to confuse us. He has introduced false concepts and doctrines into the very church itself. So let's cut through the *fake news* that Satan is pushing. Let's take a close look at some of these false ideas Satan uses to deceive, and then turn to the Bible to find what the truth really is. That's what we'll be doing in the rest of this book. We'll look at what the Bible says about some important doctrines in order to find out the truth about Satan's *fake news.*

CHAPTER 2

Is God Responsible for Both Good and Evil?

Fake News

1. There is no God; the world and those who occupy it are the result of millions, if not billions, of years of evolution.

2. There is a God, and it is His fault that sin and suffering exist, because God created everything—both good and evil.

Sometimes I look up at the moon and think, *Human beings have walked up there!* That's pretty amazing. I don't believe I have ever talked with anyone involved in the space program who wasn't excited and in awe about what we've been able to do in space.

I once spent a whole day with General Tom Stafford, the highest-ranking astronaut in the Apollo space program. He is the cousin of a friend of mine. We talked about a number of things; but no matter what the subject, it soon switched to the space program. General Stafford piloted on several moon missions. He took a photo from space that many consider to be the clearest and most beautiful picture ever made of the North American continent. (He even gave me an autographed copy.)

"You know," he told me, "when you're out there in space, looking back down to Earth, it looks like the moon, only larger. And when you're looking at Earth from that perspective, it seems like the most beautiful, peaceful thing you could possibly imagine."

That's what our world looked like from his spacecraft. But once he reached Earth again, he recognized that no matter how peaceful Earth looked from space, it was clear when up close that all was not well.

Have you ever wondered why there's so much sin and suffering in our world? Have you ever wondered why good people suffer as much as bad people? Why are innocent victims killed while the drunk driver who caused the accident walks away without a scratch? Why do earthquakes, fires, floods, and all kinds of disasters fill the news? Why are millions of people hungry and homeless? To list all of the pain and misery and horrors going on in the world today would take pages and pages.

In short, if God is so good, why do we have such a bad world? That is a question men and women have struggled with for a long, long time.

One answer some people give is that there really is no God. The world and humanity are just the result of evolution over billions of years. Suffering and misery are simply part of the way the world is. God is not responsible, because there is no God. All we can do is accept it and try to be as happy as we can.

In fact, that answer is Satan's *Fake News* no. 1. The devil would be happy for us to believe that there is no God and that our world and all of us on it are just the result of the blind, random hand of evolution. But do you know what the Bible says? "The fool has said in his heart, 'There is no God' " (Psalm 14:1). You would have to be a fool, the Bible says, to believe that God does not exist.

Yes, the world is filled with misery and suffering, but it isn't because there is no God and we're left here to cope with the bad parts of life on our own. That is *fake news*. The Bible is clear that not only does God exist, but He also created our world and everything and everyone on it. The very first words of Scripture are these: "In the beginning God created the heavens and the earth" (Genesis 1:1).

God spoke our world and the universe into existence. The Bible says, "By the word of the LORD the heavens were made, and all the host of them by the breath of His mouth. . . . He spoke, and it was done; He commanded, and it stood fast" (Psalm 33:6, 9).

But if God created everything and if He is all powerful and in control, then is He responsible for the bad as well as the good? Is it His fault there's so much suffering and misery in the world today?

Satan would love to have us believe that. This is *Fake News* no. 2: God is to blame for all the bad things that happen to us. There's no question that we live in a flawed world filled with sin and evil. But who is responsible?

The apostle Peter wrote, "Your adversary the devil walks about like a roaring lion, seeking whom he may devour" (1 Peter 5:8).

"Oh," someone says, "you believe in the devil?"

Yes, I do.

I have seen the devil work up close and personal. Once when I was holding some evangelistic meetings the pastor of the church told me, "I don't believe in the devil. I don't believe he exists."

Well, let me tell you something. When you start working for God and preaching His Word, you'll find out that the devil is real and that he is fighting against you as hard as he can. Many things happened during those evangelistic meetings to disrupt them and prevent people from hearing the truths of the Bible.

A young man who was attending those meetings had an accident and broke his arm. Another person broke his leg. One night while there was a row of cars parked along the street outside the church during the meeting, a drunk driver plowed into the last car in the row and shoved it up into the next car. That car ran into the next, which ran into the next, until he had telescoped six cars into a pile. A police officer came inside and stopped me while I was preaching. He began reading off license-plate numbers and asking if these cars belonged to people in the meeting. Sure enough, every one of those six cars belonged to someone attending the meetings. They didn't belong to people across the street or down the street but only to people inside listening to God's Word.

One lady jumped up and ran outside when she heard her license-plate number. She was excited because her poodle was in the car. She came back in carrying the dog. The police officer had already disturbed my preaching; I was not used to having that happen. Then this lady came back in with her poodle and sat down about three rows from the front, holding it. The dog kept licking her face. I don't mind admitting I had a hard time finishing my sermon that night.

So many things happened during those meetings that the pastor of that church came to me after a few weeks and said, "I've changed my mind; I believe the devil does exist!"

When we see the tracks of a deer in some mud or snow, we know a deer has been there. Even if we didn't know from Scripture that the devil is prowling around, trying to destroy and devour us, we would know he's there because we can see his tracks. The evil, sin, and suffering in the world today are the footprints of the devil.

Where did the devil come from? Did God create him? If so, isn't God responsible for evil, even if it is the devil who is the one carrying it out?

Jesus said, "I saw Satan fall like lightning from heaven" (Luke 10:18). Now that's a strange place for the devil to come from, isn't it? Many people think the devil came from hell. But that's not what the Bible says. It says that the devil, Satan, came from heaven!

Did God create the devil? Is that why he was in heaven?

No. God did not create the devil. Satan was once a perfect, beautiful angel in heaven. He was called Lucifer then. God created him "full of wisdom and perfect in beauty" but Lucifer turned himself into the devil (Ezekiel 28:12). God was not to blame. The Bible says of Lucifer, "You were perfect in your ways from the day you were created, till iniquity was found in you" (verse 15).

What happened to turn this perfect angel into the devil himself?

Lucifer allowed jealousy to fill his mind. He resented having to follow God's will and became proud of his beauty and wisdom (see verse 17). Eventually, he came to believe he should take God's place. The Bible says of him, "You have said in your heart, 'I will . . . exalt my throne above the stars of God; . . . I will be like the Most High' " (Isaiah 14:13, 14).

Lucifer wanted to unseat God and take His place on the throne of heaven. Lucifer's rebellion reached the point of war in heaven itself. Lucifer and the angels who joined his uprising against God were cast out of heaven to this earth (see Revelation 12:7–9). That's why Jesus said that He saw Satan fall from heaven like lightning.

When Satan and his angels were thrown out of

heaven to this earth, Satan continued his warfare against God by tempting Adam and Eve to distrust God and disobey Him. Of course, he was successful. Eve ate the fruit that God had commanded them not to eat. She brought some to her husband, and Adam joined her in disobeying God (see Genesis 3). Sin came into the world, and with sin came death, heartache, pain, and every kind of terrible, evil, horrible thing.

Was that God's fault? No, that was Satan's fault. Lucifer in heaven became the devil and Satan here on Earth. Sin began with him. There was no reason for him to become proud and rebellious in heaven. God created him perfect and holy. There was no flaw in God's creation of Lucifer that caused him to sin. God created a perfect being, and that perfect being chose to sin and become God's enemy. The Bible says, "[The devil] was a murderer from the beginning, and does not stand in the truth, because there is no truth in him. When he speaks a lie, he speaks from his own resources, for he is a liar and the father of it" (John 8:44).

Lucifer began his *fake-news* campaign against God in heaven. He is the father of lies. He can take something and turn it just a little until the truth becomes a lie. That's what he did in heaven. He went among the angels, raising doubts and twisting the truth just enough to deceive them into believing a lie. And ever so slowly, his *fake news* took hold until a number of the angels began to side with him against God.

Is God Responsible for Both Good and Evil?

"But," someone says, "why didn't God just nip all this in the bud? Why did He allow Satan to disrupt heaven and bring about sin? After all, God could have destroyed Satan and the disloyal angels before it ever came to the point of open warfare. That way Lucifer would never have been cast to Earth to bring sin and evil to our world. Why didn't God do that?"

Yes, God could have destroyed Satan and his angels when they raised doubts about Him and sinned against their Creator. But let's stop and think what would have happened if God had done that.

Lucifer had been going around accusing God of being unjust and unfair in requiring obedience from the angels. He said that God was arbitrary and that He couldn't be trusted. If God had destroyed Lucifer, what would the angels have thought? Lucifer was so subtle in raising doubts that the angels were confused. They loved and trusted God; but Lucifer was so persuasive that they thought maybe there was some truth to his accusations against God. If God had suddenly destroyed Lucifer to prevent him from continuing his *fake news,* the angels may have thought, *Wow! Better not question anything God does! Look what happened to Lucifer. He may have been right, but if you get out of line, God will kill you!* And the questions Lucifer had raised would have continued to fester in the minds of the angels. No one would have felt safe anymore. Sin would not have been done away with; it would have merely gone underground. Once sin arose in the mind of Lucifer, and he began to question God's love and goodness, the only way the issues could be forever settled was for God to allow sin to run its course. Everyone in the universe had to see where sin would lead. Everyone had to be convinced from the evidence that God is love and that His commandments are loving and fair. Destroying Lucifer in heaven while the questions were still unsettled would have solved nothing.

"I can see that," someone objects, "but couldn't God have created Lucifer and the angels in such a way that they *couldn't* sin? Why did God create angels and people with the ability to choose? Why didn't He create Adam and Eve so that they would always love and serve Him? Couldn't He have made it impossible for them to sin?"

I suppose He could have. But doing that would have ruined the reason God created angels and human beings in the first place. God loves us, and He wants us to love Him. Yet He wants us to do it voluntarily, not because we have to. There would be no joy in His heart if we lived in perfect obedience to His will just because we couldn't do anything else.

When my children were little, one of my greatest joys was when they came up and crawled into my lap and hugged me around the neck and said, "Daddy, I love you so much!" I never got tired of that. I always hugged them back and said, "I love you too!" That was such a wonderful feeling. It made all the difficulties and struggles of being a parent worthwhile.

But what if I knew that they didn't have a choice?

What if I knew that they loved me only because they were programmed to love me and couldn't do anything else?

Oh, their actions would have been the same. The hugs would have been just as tight. And the I love yous would have sounded the same. But it wouldn't have meant very much, would it? Is it really love if you can't do anything else? It isn't, is it?

The Bible says, "God is love" (1 John 4:8). He loves us far more than any earthly parents can love their children. He wants us to love Him in return. He wants us to love Him with all our hearts and minds. But we can't do that unless we have the ability to choose to do so. God doesn't want robots, programmed to hug His neck and tell Him how much they love Him any more than we want loving robot children. The only way to genuinely love and be loved is to be able to freely choose to love. God so loved the world that He was willing to let us choose whether to love or not to love. That's the only way we can have the relationship with God that He wants us to have.

In heaven, Lucifer was free to choose whether to love and serve God or to sin and turn away from his Creator. Sadly, he made the decision to sin. Our first parents in Eden also tragically made the decision to sin. They chose to believe Satan instead of trusting God, and that decision gave Satan his foothold in our world.

Because of that, Satan claims to be the ruler of this world, and he has continued his rebellion against God here on Earth. And that's why our world is filled with misery and suffering. God isn't responsible; Satan is. God created a perfect angel and that angel made a devil of himself. Sin and death and evil are his responsibility.

Of course, being the master of *fake news,* Satan tries to twist things so that people will believe these problems are God's fault. Insurance policies sometimes even refer to natural disasters, such as floods and fires and tornadoes, as "acts of God." They're not acts of God; they're acts of Satan. He's the one responsible.

Sometimes people say to me, "God is way off, up there in heaven. He doesn't really pay attention to the sin and terrible things that are happening on Earth."

Yes, He does. He sees it all, much more clearly than we can. He knows about these things, much more than we can, because He sees it all. It grieves Him and hurts Him far more than we can imagine. God understands the cost of sin. The Bible says, "God so loved the world that He gave His only begotten Son, that whoever believes in Him should not perish but have everlasting life" (John 3:16). Sin has cost God everything.

God did not destroy Lucifer when he rebelled in heaven because sin was still an unknown to the rest of the universe, and the only way it could be resolved forever was to allow its full results to be clearly seen. The devil won't be allowed to continue to plunge the world into sin and sorrow forever. His *fake news* against God's character and His law won't be allowed to continue forever. Sin and Satan will be destroyed. All this suffering and starvation and misery will come to an end.

Jesus Christ went to the cross to bring an end to Satan and his lies. The Bible puts it this way: Jesus became a human being like us "that through death He might destroy him who had the power of death, that is, the devil" (Hebrews 2:14). "For this purpose the Son of God was manifested, that He might destroy the works of the devil" (1 John 3:8).

The devil will be destroyed. Sin and sinners will be no more. Right now the world can be a cruel place, full of unspeakable suffering, but a day is coming when this will be over. At that time, the Bible says, "Behold, the tabernacle of God is with men, and He will dwell with them, and they shall be His people. God Himself will be with them and be their God. And God will wipe away every tear from their eyes; there shall be no more death, nor sorrow, nor crying. There shall be no more pain, for the former things have passed away" (Revelation 21:3, 4).

Wouldn't you love to live in a world like that? You can, because Jesus died on the cross not only to destroy Satan and sin but also to bring eternal life to you. A life in which there is no sorrow, no crying, no pain, and no tears. No wonder the apostle Paul wrote, "Thanks be to God for His indescribable gift!" (2 Corinthians 9:15).

God's gift of salvation and eternal life, made possible by the sacrifice of His Son, Jesus, really is indescribable. The apostle couldn't have said it any better. Oh, we can try to describe it, but it's such a great gift that we can't begin to comprehend the love that would cause the Father and Son to agree to such a sacrifice. Jesus came to our sin-darkened world to live a perfect, righteous life and die the death that we deserve—all so that we may have His righteousness and life forever with Him in heaven. Truly, that is an indescribable gift!

I've met a lot of people who are trying to earn salvation. They try with all their might to be good in their own strength and willpower, but I'm here to tell you that you can't ever be good enough to deserve salvation. That is why God offers it to you as a gift. You do not *deserve* a gift. You do not *earn* a gift. You *accept* a gift. That's what God wants you to do with the gift He offers you. Just accept it. He wants to save you, and He will—if you will just let Him. Just accept the eternal life He offers.

The apostle John says he heard God say, " 'Behold, I make all things new.' And He said to me, 'Write, for these words are true and faithful' " (Revelation 21:5). Satan's *fake news* has caused suffering and misery for centuries. But God's words are "true and faithful." He says He's going to make all things new, and He will. When Jesus comes, as He has promised, you can live with Him in that amazing new world where suffering and pain, which Satan has darkened our world with for so long, will forever be things of the past and all things will be new!

CHAPTER 3

When a Person Dies— What Then?

Fake News

1. When you die, that's it. There is no life of any kind after death. This is all there is to life, so eat, drink, and be merry, for tomorrow we die!

2. There is no death because your soul is immortal. When you die, you pass from life into eternal life—either in heaven or in hell!

My father was a creature of habit. For as long as I could remember, every Saturday night around 10:00 P.M. he would wind the clock on the mantel before going to bed.

One night my father and mother were sound asleep in bed. My younger brother and I slept in our parents room, and my two older brothers slept in another. The only other bedroom in our house belonged to our eighteen-year-old sister, Mary. She had gone out with friends that evening.

We were all sleeping soundly when the phone

rang in the hall. I heard my father quickly get out of bed and go to answer it. My mother, sensing that something must be wrong, began to pray and cry softly. I quickly crawled into bed with her.

On the phone, my father heard the terrible news. Mary had been riding in the back seat of a car with her friends. There had been a minor accident after which their car still stood in the road. Before anyone had time to get out of the car, a drunk driver traveling at high speed plowed into them. Mary and her friend in the back seat were killed.

You can imagine our shock and the horrible days that followed: first, the difficult funeral and burial; and then those lonely days after everyone had left and the family was alone. We were left with our quiet guilt: Was there something we could have done to prevent this terrible tragedy?

My father had six sisters, and a few days after the funeral, one of them called. She dabbled in spiritualism, and she told us that she had been in touch with Mary and that Mary missed us and wanted to contact Mom and Dad.

What do you do in a situation like that? Do you check it out? Was it really Mary who my aunt was contacting?

What happens when a person dies? It this all there is? Or do we continue living in some form? I suppose there are few questions through the ages that people have pondered longer and harder: *What lies on the other side of death? What will happen when I die?*

Once again, Satan is happy to introduce *fake*

news on this subject. He is very pleased with those who believe that death is the end and that there is no life beyond the grave. If this life is all there is, then why not grab the pleasure and satisfaction this world offers? Why worry about eternity if you know that you have only seventy or eighty or possibly ninety years to enjoy life before passing off the scene forever?

Many people—no matter what religious beliefs they hold—believe that when they die, they will continue their lives in some form somewhere. Many refuse to believe that this brief life is all there is. And I believe that is true—death is not the final end. But even here, Satan continues to try to deceive us with *fake news.* In fact, one of the very first lies Satan told in the Garden of Eden was on this very point.

Remember that Satan came into the Garden in the form of a serpent to tempt Eve to disobey God and eat the forbidden fruit. The conversation went like this:

Now the serpent was more cunning than any beast of the field which the LORD God had made. And he said to the woman, "Has God indeed said, 'You shall not eat of every tree of the garden'?"

And the woman said to the serpent, "We may eat the fruit of the trees of the garden; but of the fruit of the tree which is in the midst of the garden, God has said, 'You shall not eat it, nor shall you touch it, lest you die.' "

Then the serpent said to the woman, "You will not surely die" (Genesis 3:1–4).

Did you catch that? God said, "Disobey and die." But Satan said, "You will not surely die." God says, "The wages of sin is death" (Romans 6:23). But Satan says, "You will not surely die." Who is telling the truth? Who is putting out *fake news*?

Many Christians believe Satan's *fake news*. They believe that when people die, they don't really die. Instead, people—at least their souls—go on living either in heaven or hell. This whole matter of what happens when people die can be confusing. Satan has done his best to make it so. How can we know the truth?

Let's turn to the Bible, that infallible source of truth, and see what it says about what happens when a person dies. This is an important question, and the Bible will give us the truth. To understand the biblical view of death, we need to begin back at Creation. We need to see how our Creator gave us life at the beginning. Here's what the Bible says: "The LORD God formed man of the dust of the ground, and breathed into his nostrils the breath of life; and man became a living being" (Genesis 2:7).

God could have made the first human being from anything, but He chose to form Adam from "the dust of the ground." He combined all the necessary elements to form bones and flesh and nerves and muscles. But something more was needed to turn that body into a living being. The Bible says God breathed into that inanimate body "the breath of life," and Adam became a living human being! The life-giving power of God began to flow through Adam's nerves and veins and brain. As the result of that combination—the "dust of the ground" plus "the breath of life"—Adam "became a living being" ("a living soul" [Genesis 2:7, KJV]).

Notice that the Bible says Adam *became* a living soul, not that he *received* a soul. As we will see, the Bible doesn't support the idea that we humans have some vague, spiritlike component called a soul. The Bible typically uses the term *soul* to mean a living person—the same thing we mean when we say, "By the time we arrived, there wasn't a soul there," meaning everyone had left before we got there.

We can describe the process in Genesis by which God created human life almost like a math formula:

dust of the ground + breath of life =
a living being (soul)

The Bible explains what happens at death as the reverse of this process. "Then the dust will return to the earth as it was, and the spirit will return to God who gave it" (Ecclesiastes 12:7). According to the Bible, when a person dies, his or her body (the dust) returns to the ground (decays), and the spirit (the breath of life) returns to its source—God. It's the reverse of the creative process in Genesis. We can write this formula as the following:

dust of the ground – breath of life =
a dead being (soul)

It's similar to what happens when you turn off a lamp. A lightbulb plus electricity equals light. But where does the light go when you turn off the electricity? It doesn't go anywhere; it simply ceases to exist. When the breath of life is disconnected from the body at death, where does the "soul" go? It doesn't go anywhere; it simply ceases to exist. That person is no longer a living being, or a "living soul." When we're alive, we are living beings; but in death, we're simply lifeless bodies—corpses. When God takes back the breath of life He gave us, our "souls" no longer exists.

"Wait a minute," I can hear someone say. "The text says that at death 'the spirit will return to God.' That means when a person dies, the soul goes to heaven and lives there forever with God."

Let's look a little more closely at that. Many Christians believe that we all have an immortal soul that goes on living, either in heaven or in hell, after the body dies. But is that what the Bible teaches?

In Ezekiel, God says this about the soul: " 'As I live,' says the Lord GOD. . . . 'Behold, all souls are Mine; . . . the soul who sins shall die' " (Ezekiel 18:3, 4). Here the Bible is using the word *soul* to mean a human being. In fact, nowhere in the Bible does it say that we have an immortal soul. The Hebrew and Greek words for *soul*, *spirit*, and *breath* occur in the Bible some seventeen hundred times, and not once do they refer to the human soul, spirit, or breath as being immortal. Nowhere in the Bible does it state that human beings have any conscious existence apart from the body. The Bible is clear that in this life we are mortal, subject to death. It says that only God is immortal (1 Timothy 6:15, 16).

It's true that when Jesus comes again, our mortal nature will experience an amazing transformation. Speaking of the righteous when Jesus returns, the apostle Paul writes, "We shall all be changed—in a moment, in the twinkling of an eye, at the last trumpet. For the trumpet will sound, and the dead will be raised incorruptible, and we shall be changed. For this corruptible must put on incorruption, and this mortal must put on immortality. So when this corruptible has put on incorruption, and this mortal has put on immortality, then shall be brought to pass the saying that is written: 'Death is swallowed up in victory' " (1 Corinthians 15:51–54).

We're not immortal now, but we have God's promise that we will become immortal when Jesus returns and we will live with Him forever! God will give us the gift of immortality.

Let's look further at what the Bible says about death. It says that dead people aren't aware of anything happening on earth. They know nothing. They have no contact with the living.

For the living know that they will die; but the dead know nothing, and they have no more reward, for the memory of them is forgotten. Also their love, their hatred, and their envy have now perished; nevermore will they have a share in anything done under the sun. . . .

Whatever your hand finds to do, do it with your might; for there is no work or device or knowledge or wisdom in the grave where you are going (Ecclesiastes 9:5, 6, 10).

That's pretty clear, isn't it? The dead know nothing. They have no more involvement in anything done under the sun. Death is like a deep, dreamless sleep. The psalmist wrote, "For in death there is no remembrance of You [God]; in the grave who will give You thanks?" (Psalm 6:5).

The Bible teaches that when people die, they are truly dead. Their thoughts perish. They rest in the grave unaware of anything—until God calls them forth in the resurrection. Jesus said, "The hour is coming in which all who are in the graves will hear His [God's] voice and come forth—those who have done good, to the resurrection of life, and those who have done evil, to the resurrection of condemnation" (John 5:28, 29). Until then, those who have died—both the righteous and the wicked—rest in their graves. The wicked do not go to hell at death, and the righteous do not go to heaven when they die. The dead rest unconscious in their graves.

Now, if that is true—and it is, because the Bible says it is—what about mediums who claim to contact the dead and speak with them? Is that possible, if what the Bible says is true? No. Contacting the dead through spirit mediums is just another part of Satan's *fake news* about death.

I was seven years old when my sister Mary died. I mentioned earlier that my aunt, one of my dad's sisters, called to tell us that through a spiritualist medium she had been in contact with Mary and that Mary wanted to get in touch with Mom and Dad.

My father belonged to a popular Protestant church that taught the spirits of dead people live on either in heaven or in hell. He missed Mary terribly, as did my mother. He was ready and willing to work with my aunt to try to contact Mary. But Mother was a student of God's Word, and her church believed what the Bible taught about death: the dead know nothing and can have nothing to do with the living while they sleep in the grave. Mother was not deceived by Satan's *fake news* about death. She told my aunt, "You know I love you, and I believe you are sincere. But you haven't been talking to Mary. The Bible says that the dead know nothing."

There is a lot of interest today in mediums, spiritualism, and contacting the dead. That's because so many have bought into Satan's *fake news* that the soul is immortal and lives on after death. If that were true, it would be logical for the dead to try to contact their living loved ones. If the living believe their loved ones still live on in some way, no wonder people try to get in touch with those who have died. But what does the Bible say about seeking the dead through spirit mediums?

"And when they say to you, 'Seek those who are mediums and wizards, who whisper and mutter,' should not a people seek their God? Should they seek the dead on behalf of the living?" (Isaiah 8:19). The Bible is clear that we are to avoid mediums who claim to be able to contact the dead. We are to have nothing to do with them (Leviticus 19:31; 20:6). The reason is that when we try to contact the dead, we are putting ourselves in Satan's hands. Satan and his angels are at work to deceive. They impersonate our dead loved ones and trick sincere people into believing that they are speaking with people they love who have died. It is all part of Satan's *fake news* about death. We should not wonder at this, for the Bible says Satan "transforms himself into an angel of light" (2 Corinthians 11:14). He is a master of deception and *fake news*.

"But," someone says, "I heard my loved one's voice!" Did you ever watch a comedian impersonate a president of the United States? The comedian's voice sounded exactly like the person he was impersonating! Some Elvis impersonators are so good at sounding like him that we are astounded! Yes, it's not difficult for the devil to deceive "even the elect," the Bible says (Matthew 24:24). The Bible's clear, consistent teaching about death is that the dead rest unconscious in the grave. The wicked don't go to hell at death, and the righteous don't go to heaven when they die. Both wait in the grave until the resurrection—either the resurrection of life or the resurrection of condemnation (John 5:28, 29).

God's way is always the best way. Think of what it would mean if a righteous person went to heaven when he or she died, as so many Christians believe. Suppose a godly mother dies and goes to heaven. According to the usual understanding, she can look down on Earth and see everything that is going on. She is a young mother and leaves her husband a widower and a six-month-old baby boy without his mother. She watches from heaven over the next months and years as her husband tries to take care of that child by himself.

Suppose the boy grows up to get in trouble with the law, and his mother in heaven sees him get arrested for murder. Or she watches as he becomes an alcoholic or a drug addict. Or maybe he is stricken with cancer and suffers terribly. The mother is aware of all this, yet heaven is supposed to be a happy place where there are no tears or sorrow of any kind. What would heaven be like for this poor mother? Could she enjoy eternal life in heaven under these circumstances? Could she watch the tragedy and heartache through which her son and husband pass without her own heart being broken with sorrow? No mother who has ever lived could watch such things without suffering along with her loved ones on Earth.

Thank God that isn't His plan! Thank God that death is a peaceful, quiet sleep in which the dead know nothing! It's a comfort to know that our dead loved ones are resting in the grave, unaware of what is happening on Earth.

The dead are truly dead, but the grave is not the end of the story. "Jesus said to her, 'I am the resurrection and the life. He who believes in Me, though he may die, he shall live' " (John 11:25). Our loved ones who have died in Christ sleep in the grave, waiting for His voice to raise them to life once again. The apostle Paul assures us that we can trust God's promise of a glorious resurrection to eternal life for those who love Him.

> But I do not want you to be ignorant, brethren, concerning those who have fallen asleep, lest you sorrow as others who have no hope. For if we believe that Jesus died and rose again, even so God will bring with Him those who sleep in Jesus.
>
> For this we say to you by the word of the Lord, that we who are alive and remain until the coming of the Lord will by no means precede those who are asleep. For the Lord Himself will descend from heaven with a shout, with the voice of an archangel, and with the trumpet of God. And the dead in Christ will rise first. Then we who are alive and remain shall be caught up together with them in the clouds to meet the Lord in the air. And thus we shall always be with the Lord. Therefore comfort one another with these words (1 Thessalonians 4:13–18).

Years and years may pass between the time a

godly person dies in Christ and the resurrection morning Paul is describing here. But to that person asleep in the grave, it will seem like only a moment. One moment his eyes close in death, and the next he sees Jesus coming in the clouds of glory!

Recently, I got up early in the morning to run an errand in a nearby town. On the return trip, I received a call from my son-in-law with a very short message. "Dad," he said, "please come! We just got word that Ben has been killed in an auto accident."

Ben is my grandson. I immediately headed that direction as a flood of tears rolled down my face and an anguished cry came from my lips. Arriving at the house, I found my daughter, Maryann, and her husband, Kirk, surrounded by their friends. Their grief was deep, and the tears flowed freely as they and Ben's four sisters—Katie, Camille, Venice, and Carrie—held each other and cried. My wife Camille and I are very close to our four children and to our grandchildren. Ben had lived with us when he was working at 3ABN, and I have spent more time with him than with any of the other grandchildren. Ben had loved Jesus from the time of his childhood and had recently moved into a deeper experience with the Lord.

The memorial service was difficult for Maryann, Kirk, and the family. Ben had so many friends; some flew hundreds of miles to be there for the family. Other friends from 3ABN, such as Danny Shelton, C. A. and Irma Murray, and Shelley and J. D. Quinn, sent videos. Reggie and Ladye Love

Smith sent a personal testimony video about how Ben had been an influence for good on their son Brett. Reggie also sent a hymn that he had just recorded with the Gaither Vocal Band.

My mother had five children—four sons and one daughter—and lost her daughter, Mary, in an auto accident. My daughter, Maryann, who was named for my sister, Mary, had four daughters and one son, and now she had lost him in an auto accident. What a heartbreaking situation for those two mothers and fathers, for the siblings, and for both sets of grandparents.

But thank God that is not the end! The truth about death is so much more comforting than the devil's *fake news*! For God's children, a day is coming when there will be no more death or sorrow or crying. God says He will wipe all tears from our eyes and make all things new (see Revelation 21:4, 5). We will have our loved ones again—not just for a night but forever! On that glorious resurrection morning, Paul says,

"Death is swallowed up in victory."
  "O Death, where is your sting? . . ."
  The sting of death is sin. . . . But thanks be to God, who gives us the victory through our Lord Jesus Christ (1 Corinthians 15:54–57).

That's God's good news for you and me!

CHAPTER 4

Are Sinners Burning in Hell Today?

Fake News

1. There is no such thing as hell. Hell is just something religion has invented in order to control people.

2. Hell is a real place where people are being tortured right now in eternal flames of burning fire. Hell lasts forever and ever; it will never end!

I was making a pastoral call one day at an apartment building. As I walked up to the entryway, I noticed two little girls tormenting a third girl. "You keep acting like that," one of the tormentors was saying, "and you will end up in hell. It's horrible there."

"Yeah," agreed the second tormentor. "God will send you to hell where you'll burn forever and ever and ever. But you won't ever burn up. You'll just keep burning and burning. There'll be flames everywhere."

By this time, the third little girl was in tears. Of course, she was. Wouldn't you be crying at the thought of screaming in horrible agony—burning forever but never burning up? I know I would.

Do you think what that little girl heard about hell made her love God? I doubt it. How could anyone love a God who would burn people for eternity to punish them for the sins of a brief lifetime?

But that is exactly what many Christians believe. Through the centuries, theologians and preachers have had some amazing things to say about hell. Some have taught that babies who die without being baptized go to hell, where they are engulfed in flames and their blood runs through their veins like molten lead! One common view pictures the devil going around with a red-hot poker, pressing it against the bare feet of sinners. Eighteenth-century preacher Jonathan Edwards delivered a sermon titled "Sinners in the Hands of an Angry God." Here is part of what he had to say in that sermon:

> Men are held in the Hand of God over the Pit of Hell. . . .
>
> God . . . holds you over the Pit of Hell, much as one holds a Spider, or some loathsome Insect, over the Fire, [he] abhors you, and is dreadfully provoked; his Wrath towards you burns like Fire; he looks upon you as worthy of nothing else, but to be cast into the Fire; he is of purer Eyes than to bear to have you in his Sight; you are ten thousand Times so abominable in his Eyes as the most hateful venomous Serpent is in ours. . . .
>
> O Sinner! Consider the fearful Danger you

are in: 'Tis a great Furnace of Wrath, a wide and bottomless Pit, full of the Fire of Wrath, that you are held over in the Hand of that God. . . : You hang by a slender Thread, with the Flames of divine Wrath flashing about it, and ready every Moment to singe it, and burn it asunder. . . .

'Tis everlasting Wrath. It would be dreadful to suffer this Fierceness and Wrath of Almighty God one moment; but you must suffer it to all Eternity: there will be no End to this exquisite horrible Misery.[1]

We've seen how Satan is continuously putting out *fake news* about God. Is this idea about an eternally burning hell part of his *fake-news* campaign? If so, it would certainly be an effective way to turn people away from God. How many people have rejected God because they couldn't love and serve a God who would burn people alive in hell for all eternity?

For these folks, Satan has introduced his *Fake News* no. 1. He tells people, "There is no such thing as hell. Hell is just something religion has invented to scare and control people into being good." The problem with that *fake news* is that the Bible definitely does talk about hell. The Bible definitely does teach that unrepentant sinners will be punished for their sins.

So Satan thought up *Fake News* no. 2 about hell, causing people to believe that hell is a real place where people are being tortured right now in eternal flames of burning fire. And this hell, Satan teaches, lasts forever; it will never end.

We'll see what the Bible says about hell—what it is and when it begins and how long it lasts. And I promise you that the biblical view of hell is not the same as Satan's *fake news* about hell. But before we look at what the Bible says, let's ask a question: Is the idea of an eternally burning hell logical or just?

In the first place, such a teaching is not a teaching of love, and God is love (1 John 4:8). It is utterly impossible to reconcile the idea of a loving God with the belief that He tosses His created children into a fire that never stops burning. I do not know anyone on earth who could do that. Neither do you.

In early January 2015, the world was horrified when radical extremists in the Middle East put captured Jordanian pilot Muath Safi Yousef al-Kasasbeh in an iron cage and burned him alive. This atrocity provoked widespread outrage around the world. Yet as sickening as this terrible tragedy was, it pales in comparison to what many Christians believe God will do to unrepentant sinners. Can we truly believe that a God of love would punish someone for trillions upon trillions of unending years because of a brief lifetime of sin?

There are sincere people on both sides of the debate about the death penalty for certain crimes. Some feel that capital punishment should be abolished entirely. But even those who favor the death penalty agree that it should be carried out as swiftly and as humanely as possible. No matter how heinous the crime, no one suggests that we should torture the guilty person. No one argues that we should burn convicted criminals in a fire designed to keep them alive as long as possible in order to bring about the greatest agony. Yet that is the *fake news* that Satan is spreading about God!

Is Satan's *fake news* about hell even logical or just?

The Bible is clear that God has a Judgment Day at the end of time when people's lives will be examined and their final fate determined. "We must all appear before the judgment seat of Christ, that each one may receive the things done in the body, according to what he has done, whether good or bad," wrote the apostle Paul (2 Corinthians 5:10). "And as it is appointed for men to die once, but after this the judgment" (Hebrews 9:27). But if sinners were thrown into hell at death, as is widely believed, God would be guilty of executing punishment upon sinners without a trial before the day of judgment. Would that be just and fair? If men and women are sent to their reward or punishment when they die, what need is there for a later judgment to determine their guilt or innocence? God would never punish sinners before the judgment. That wouldn't be fair at all. So we can rest assured that no one is burning in hell today.

To consign sinners to never-ending flames when they die would be grossly unfair and certainly not worthy of a just God. For example, Cain killed one man—his brother. That would mean that

Cain has been suffering in agony in hell now for approximately six thousand years. Yet some modern mass murderer who has killed multiple individuals can never catch up with Cain in the amount of punishment, even though both of them would burn throughout eternity. Cain would always have received six thousand more years of punishment for murdering one person than would the mass murderer. Are we willing to attribute such an injustice to God?

Satan's *fake news* about hell requires that we view God as unjust, unfair, and more cruel than we can possibly imagine any human being. Fortunately, when we turn to the Bible and see what God's Word has to say about hell, we find a very different picture than Satan is painting with his *fake news*. " 'As I live,' says the Lord GOD, 'I have no pleasure in the death of the wicked, but that the wicked turn from his way and live. Turn, turn from your evil ways! For why should you die, O house of Israel?' " (Ezekiel 33:11). The apostle Peter wrote, "The Lord . . . is longsuffering toward us, not willing that any should perish" (2 Peter 3:9).

God doesn't want anyone to be lost and end up in hell. He loved the world so much that He gave His only Son, Jesus Christ, to die in our place so that we could be saved (John 3:16).

So how did Satan deceive people into believing his *fake news*?

Satan's *fake news* about hell grew out of his *fake news* about death. As we've seen, Satan has succeeded in convincing almost everyone that when people die, they don't really die, and instead, we all have an immortal soul that cannot die. If that's true, if people go on living after death (and according to the Bible, they don't), then they must live somewhere. So Satan put out the idea that when people die, the righteous dead go to heaven and the wicked go to hell.

From the beginning of his rebellion, Satan has charged that God is an unjust tyrant, not a God of love. Hell, if it exists as Satan's *fake news* portrays it, would be convincing evidence that Satan's accusations against God are true.

"But," someone says, "hell must be real because the Bible talks about it. Jesus Himself warned us to beware of hell."

That is true. But let's see what the Bible really says about hell and whether it matches Satan's *fake news* at all.

What does the Bible say about the punishment of the wicked? "The Lord knoweth how to deliver the godly out of temptations, and to reserve the unjust unto the day of judgment to be punished" (2 Peter 2:9, KJV).

Are the wicked being punished in hell now for their sins? No. The Bible says that God is reserving the unjust "unto the day of judgment to be punished." Contrary to Satan's *fake news,* there is no hellfire burning today into which sinners go when they die.

In Revelation, the apostle John describes events

taking place a thousand years after Christ's second coming. He wrote, "Then I saw a great white throne and Him [God] who sat on it. . . . And I saw the dead, small and great, standing before God, and books were opened. And another book was opened, which is the Book of Life. And the dead were judged according to their works, by the things which were written in the books. . . . And they were judged, each one according to his works. . . . And anyone not found written in the Book of Life was cast into the lake of fire" (Revelation 20:11–13, 15).

John describes the final attempt by Satan and the wicked to overthrow God. He wrote, "They [the wicked] went up on the breadth of the earth and surrounded the camp of the saints and the beloved city. And fire came down from God out of heaven and devoured them. The devil, who deceived them, was cast into the lake of fire and brimstone" (verses 9, 10).

This text answers several of our questions about hell. What is hell? It is the fire that God rains down on sinners at the end of time to destroy them. Where is hell? Hell will take place right here on this earth. When is hell? Hell will take place at the end of time after the final judgment by God on His great white throne.

How long will hell burn? Did you notice what John wrote about the hellfire that falls on the wicked? John wrote, "And fire came down from God out of heaven *and devoured them*" (verse 9; emphasis added). Does that sound like fire that is eternal? When something is devoured by fire, it is burned up. The fire that punishes the wicked destroys them completely.

"Wait a minute," someone replies. "You left out part of what John said about this fire. Verse 10 says that this fire continues 'forever and ever.' Doesn't that prove that hell never ends and that sinners are punished throughout eternity?"

That's a fair question. The Bible does talk about "everlasting fire" (Matthew 25:41) and describes hell as "forever." But we need to look at everything the Bible says about hell. It is always dangerous to build a doctrine on a few isolated texts instead of looking at the total picture given in the Bible.

Let's look at some of the texts in the Bible that describe the fate of the wicked. "The wicked shall be cut off" (Psalm 37:28). "Into smoke they shall vanish away" (verse 20). They shall "utterly perish" (2 Peter 2:12). They "shall be utterly destroyed" (Acts 3:23).

The prophet Malachi says this about the destruction of the wicked at the end of time: " 'For behold, the day is coming, burning like an oven, and all the proud, yes, all who do wickedly will be stubble. And the day which is coming shall burn them up,' says the LORD of hosts, 'that will leave them neither root nor branch. . . . For they shall be ashes under the soles of your feet on the day that I do this,' says the LORD of hosts" (Malachi 4:1, 3).

Jesus said, "Do not fear those who kill the body but cannot kill the soul. But rather fear Him who is able to destroy both soul and body in hell"

(Matthew 10:28). So according to Jesus, sinners are completely destroyed in hell—both soul and body. They vanish away like smoke. They become ashes.

Romans 6:23 says, "The wages of sin is death"— not eternal life in hell. Throughout the Bible, the contrast between righteousness and sin is always described as the contrast between life and death, not between eternal life in heaven and eternal life in hell. The purpose of hell—the lake of fire—is to rid the universe of sin, not to preserve sin forever as sinners suffer endlessly.

But what about those texts that seem to some to suggest an eternally burning hell—a hell that lasts forever? Many Christians agree that the idea of sinners burning in hell forever and ever is a horrible, terrible thing to consider, but they see no way to avoid it because of the way certain texts in the Bible have been interpreted.

One such text is Matthew 25:41: "Then He [God] will also say to those on the left hand, 'Depart from Me, you cursed, into the everlasting fire.' " That certainly sounds like hellfire lasts forever. But just a few verses later Jesus refers to this fire as "everlasting punishment" (verse 46). The punishment is indeed everlasting.

But punishment is not necessarily the same as *punishing*. What does the Bible say the punishment for sin is? "For the wages of sin is death." The punishment (death) will last forever. The fires of hell result in everlasting death or destruction (see 2 Thessalonians 1:9).

Are Sinners Burning in Hell Today?

Jude 7 uses the fate of Sodom and Gomorrah as an example of the fate of the wicked. It says they suffered "the vengeance of eternal fire." Obviously, those cities are not still burning today. Peter points out that God turned "the cities of Sodom and Gomorrah into ashes, [and] condemned them to destruction, making them an example to those who afterward would live ungodly" (2 Peter 2:6). The fire that burned Sodom and Gomorrah is "eternal fire" in that its consequence—permanent destruction—is eternal. But it is not eternal in the sense that it lasts forever. As Peter says, those cities were destroyed, burned to ashes—destroyed forever.

But what about those texts that speak of hell lasting forever? Revelation 14:11 says, "And the smoke of their torment ascends forever and ever." That certainly sounds like endless suffering. But let's remember that Revelation is filled with vivid, symbolic language; it's easy to misunderstand if we take it too literally. The Bible often uses the word *forever* in the same way we do. When we say, "I will remember your kindness forever," we don't literally mean we'll remember for all eternity—millions and trillions of years into the future. We mean we will remember as long as we live—as long we are able to remember.

When the prophet Isaiah described God's judgment on the wicked nation of Edom, he wrote, "Its land shall become burning pitch. It shall not be quenched night or day; its smoke shall ascend forever" (Isaiah 34:9, 10). Yet Edom is not still burning today; its

51

fires went out long ago. The Bible is using descriptive language to emphasize the complete, utter, permanent destruction that would befall Edom.

Exodus 21:6 describes piercing a servant's ear as a sign that he was to serve his master "forever"— obviously meaning as long as the servant lives. Jonah said that he was in the belly of the fish "forever" (Jonah 2:6), which Matthew 12:40 defines as three days and nights.

So when the Bible describes the fire that destroys the wicked as continuing "forever," we need to put that beside the verses that clearly indicate that the fires of hell will completely destroy the wicked and burn them up so that they never live again. Saying that "the smoke of their torment ascends forever and ever" is a vivid way of describing the eternal destruction of the wicked (Revelation 14:11). Revelation 21:8 plainly says that the lake of fire "is the second death."

Satan's *fake news* paints a picture of God as a cruel tyrant who will punish sinners with unspeakable, unending torture in hell. But when we see all that the Bible has to say about this topic, we see a God who is just and loving; a God who pleads with us to come to Him and have eternal life; and a God who gave Himself on the cross so that we might not have to suffer the just penalty of our sins. God must deal fully and finally with sin in order to cleanse the universe for all time and ensure that sin will never infect His creation again. The Bible says God "will make an utter end of it [sin]. Affliction will not rise up a second time" (Nahum 1:9).

Sin will never arise again, not because we *can't* sin, but because we won't *want* to sin. The Cross will have taught us the horrible nature and consequences of sin. The Cross will have made the universe safe from sin, and the Cross will keep it safe.

Sin and sinners will come to their end. Hell will end. The fires of hell will burn up sin, sinners, and this old world of evil. Peter wrote, "But the day of the Lord will come as a thief in the night, in which the heavens will pass away with a great noise, and the elements will melt with fervent heat; both the earth and the works that are in it will be burned up. . . . The heavens will be dissolved, being on fire, and the elements will melt with fervent heat[.] Nevertheless we, according to His promise, look for new heavens and a new earth in which righteousness dwells" (2 Peter 3:10, 12, 13).

The apostle John adds,

> Now I saw a new heaven and a new earth, for the first heaven and the first earth had passed away. . . . And God will wipe away every tear from their eyes; there shall be no more death, nor sorrow, nor crying. There shall be no more pain, for the former things have passed away.
>
> Then He who sat on the throne said, "Behold, I make all things new" (Revelation 21:1, 4, 5).

God has done everything He possibly can to

draw men and women to Him so that they can be a part of the wonderful new world He will create after sin and sinners are destroyed. He doesn't want anyone to miss out. He wants you to be there.

---

1. Jonathan Edwards, "Sinners in the Hands of an Angry God," sermon, July 8, 1741, Enfield, Connecticut, https://digitalcommons.unl.edu/cgi/viewcontent.cgi?article =1053&context=etas.

CHAPTER 5

God's Ten-Commandment Law

Fake News

1. God's so-called law is just a human invention and doesn't have any divine authority for anyone.

2. God gave the law to His people in Old Testament times, but it was done away with when Jesus died on the cross, and Christians today are not under the law but under grace.

The summer before my sophomore year in college, I sold sewing machines for Hub Appliances in Dallas, Texas. Mr. Morgan, the owner, gave me a few days off, and a friend and I went to Brackettville, Texas, where we'd heard a movie was being filmed. It was titled *The Alamo*. The movie crew had built a replica of the Alamo on the James T. Shahan ranch. My friend and I checked into a motel comprised of buildings that had once housed the famous Fort Clark.

In spite of the fact that filmmaking was in progress, there didn't seem to be much going on. People loitered around the small motel lobby. One very tall man played at the single pinball machine. I watched him until he turned and asked, "Would you like to play me a game?"

"Sure," I answered, and we played a game. In fact, we ended up playing several games.

Afterward another man said to me, "Do you know who you were playing pinball with?"

"No, I don't," I replied truthfully.

"Well, that's John Wayne," he told me.

If you know anything about John Wayne, you know he was a tough guy in the movies but generally a good guy as well. His movies often contained violence, but John Wayne's character was usually on the side of justice and right. Movies back then contained violence but not to the degree we see in films today.

These days movies are filled with killings and graphic violence of all kinds. Of course, it's make-believe. But as real violence and mass shootings and crime become more prevalent in society, people are beginning to question whether the violence in Hollywood and in computer games is inspiring the violence in real life.

Murder, rape, burglary, road rage, shootings, and all kinds of lawlessness fill the news. Did you know that according to the U.S. Bureau of Justice Statistics, less than half of the violent crime in the United States (42 percent)[1] is even reported to the police? And law-enforcement agencies nationwide solve less than half (45.6 percent) of the crimes that *are* reported.[2] No wonder crime seems out of control today!

Most of us have come in contact with crime of some kind or know someone who has. I have one friend whose auto was stolen and used as a getaway vehicle for a bank robbery! Another friend was shocked when he returned home to discover all his furniture gone. A pastor friend of mine was robbed at gunpoint.

Even churches are targets for shootings, as we have seen in South Carolina and Texas. Church burglaries are common. Convenience-store clerks are in constant danger not only of being robbed but also of being murdered, especially if they resist or recognize the robber. Law-enforcement agencies try their best to contain crime, but conditions are becoming worse and worse.

Why? What is the basic cause? Many people point fingers at drugs, alcohol, deteriorating family life, poverty, or the prevalence of guns. These are contributing factors. Yet I would suggest the real cause is deeper.

If you investigate further, you soon discover that society's regard for morals, ethics, rules, and law is crumbling in today's world. Standards of upright conduct have almost vanished. We can see this in areas other than violence and crime. Premarital sex is commonplace, with an estimated 39.8 percent of all births in the United States taking place outside marriage.[3] Corruption and fraud in business and politics are rampant. We expect our politicians to lie to us.

What is causing this breakdown in society?

The root cause is simply this: our generation has largely discarded God's standards and set up its own standards. People have dismissed God's Ten-Commandment law as too old fashioned for our modern world, and Satan is right there in the middle of it, peddling his *fake news* about God's commandments. To the nonreligious, Satan says, "God's so-called law is just a human invention; it doesn't have divine authority for anyone." This *fake news* is eagerly accepted by those who don't want to believe there are *any* divine constraints on their behavior. God's rules are irrelevant and do not apply to them.

Satan has an even more subtle form of *fake news* for those of us who acknowledge God's role in our lives. In many Christian churches, you'll hear that the Ten Commandments have been done away with. This form of Satan's *fake news* says, "God gave the law to His people in Old Testament times, but it was done away with when Jesus died on the cross. Christians today are not under the law anymore but under grace."

This is in line with the *fake news* that Satan spread in heaven when he was persuading the angels to rebel against God. "Angels don't need laws," he told them. "God is unjust in requiring obedience. God wants you to obey just to show that He is the boss."

Some time ago I went with a small group of people to an airport in Jerusalem and flew to the Sinai Peninsula. We landed and got on a bus, where we drove across the Sinai Desert, which is some of the most desolate country you'll find anywhere. We eventually arrived at Saint Catherine's Monastery, which is located right at the foot of Mount Sinai.

It was impressive to be at the base of Mount Sinai and look up the mountain toward where God Himself came down and gave Moses the Ten Commandments, written on stone tablets with His own finger. As impressive as it was to be there, though, I couldn't help thinking about what it must have been like when the children of Israel were actually camped around that spot and saw it happening before their eyes.

Here is what the Bible says: "Now Mount Sinai was completely in smoke, because the LORD descended upon it in fire. Its smoke ascended like the smoke of a furnace, and the whole mountain quaked greatly. And when the blast of the trumpet sounded long and became louder and louder, Moses spoke, and God answered him by voice. Then the LORD came down upon Mount Sinai, on the top of the mountain. And the LORD called Moses to the top of the mountain, and Moses went up" (Exodus 19:18–20).

Up on the mountain, God gave Moses the Ten Commandments. These ten simple, clear rules for living cover all the areas of our lives. They spell out how God wants us to live in our relationship with Him and with each other. They describe what God is like and what He wants us to be like.

After visiting Mount Sinai, I boarded the bus

and made my way back to Jerusalem—to the city of Mount Calvary.

Two mountains, Sinai and Calvary—the law and the Cross. Sinai tells me that God's law is important, and Calvary tells me that I have a Savior who saves me from my sins against that law. Jesus came to Earth as a human being to live a life of complete obedience to the Father's will—His commandments. Jesus died on the cross in order to cover me with His righteousness. Many sincere Christians today have bought into Satan's *fake news* that the Ten Commandments have been done away with on this side of the cross. "Since the cross," they say, "we are not under the law but under grace." But what does the Bible say?

The apostle John wrote this about God's people: "Here is the patience of the saints; here are those who keep the commandments of God and the faith of Jesus" (Revelation 14:12). Here we have *both* law and grace. It's not law *or* grace; it's law *and* grace.

Any Bible student knows that you have a serious problem if you begin doing away with God's law, because if you get rid of the law, you get rid of sin. The Bible says, "Sin is the transgression of the law" (1 John 3:4, KJV). And Paul writes, "Where there is no law there is no transgression" (Romans 4:15).

If you have ever been on an autobahn in Germany, you know that people drive differently there than in the United States. And by "differently" I mean faster—a lot faster. I found this out firsthand. A driver picked me up at the airport to take me to a meeting. I got in the car, and he took off. The fence posts went by very rapidly. I asked him how fast we were going, and he told me in kilometers.

"How fast is that in miles?" I wanted to know.

He said, "Right now, we're going one hundred and forty-five miles per hour."

He was a good driver, and the roads there are built to handle this kind of speed. But 145 miles per hour? I had never been in a car going that fast before. He wasn't breaking any laws because there are no speed limits on that particular road in Germany. He could drive as fast as he wanted.

In the United States, speed limits are around sixty-five miles per hour. In Germany, people drive through car washes at sixty-five miles per hour! If you were to drive 145 miles per hour in the United States, you'd definitely be breaking the law—but not in Germany.

Without law, the Bible says, there is no sin. We can understand that even in our everyday lives. And if there is no sin, then there is no need for a Savior. How, then, has Satan been able to convince so many Christians to believe his *fake news* that God's law was done away with after the cross?

It comes down to a misunderstanding of something the apostle Paul wrote in his letter to the Roman Christians. Paul was emphasizing that we're saved not by good works and obedience to the law but only by God's grace and the righteousness of Jesus, our Savior (Romans 3). As he developed his argument, he wrote, "Sin shall not have dominion over you, for you are not under law but under grace" (Romans 6:14).

What did he mean by that? Did he mean that God's law has been abolished and that Christians no longer need to pay any attention to it or obey it? Not at all. In fact, he dealt with that mistaken idea in the very next verse. He must have realized that people might misunderstand what he was saying.

In verse 15, Paul continues, "What then? Shall we sin because we are not under law but under grace? Certainly not!" When Paul says that Christians are not under law but under grace, he means that we are saved by the grace of God and not by our obedience to the law. But he hastens to make it clear that Christians who have been saved by God's grace won't allow sin to "have dominion" over them. They still keep God's law through the power of Jesus working in their lives. They still recognize the importance of obeying God's Ten Commandments.

The Bible says, "All his [God's] commandments are sure. They stand fast for ever and ever" (Psalm 111:7, 8, KJV). Jesus said, "Do not think that I came to destroy the Law or the Prophets. I did not come to destroy but to fulfill. For assuredly, I say to you, till heaven and earth pass away, one jot or one tittle will by no means pass from the law till all is fulfilled. Whoever therefore breaks one of the least of these commandments, and teaches men so, shall be called least in the kingdom of heaven; but whoever does and teaches them, he shall be called great in the kingdom of heaven" (Matthew 5:17–19).

Some people believe that in this verse to fulfill means to abolish or destroy. But that doesn't make any sense; Jesus would be saying, "Do not think that I came to destroy the law but to destroy it."

What Jesus meant was that He had come to fulfill the law by keeping it. He meant He came to fulfill the law by filling it full of meaning and showing its importance. He says God's law will last as long as heaven and the earth remain. Heaven and the earth are still here, aren't they? So the law is still here as well, according to Jesus.

In Romans 7, Paul stresses that God's law is "holy and just and good" (verse 12). This is in harmony with what the Bible says elsewhere about the law:

- The statutes of the LORD are right, rejoicing the heart; the commandment of the LORD is pure, enlightening the eyes (Psalm 19:8, KJV).
- I will delight myself in Your commandments, which I love (Psalm 119:47).
- All Your commandments are truth (verse 151).
- All Your commandments are righteousness (verse 172).

Satan's *fake news* about God's law has caused many Christians to view the law as something negative—something that is opposed to Christian freedom and grace. Satan has also used his *fake news* about the commandments to deceive us into believing that salvation depends on obedience. The idea that God's Ten-Commandment law has been done away with since the Cross rests on confusion over what the purpose of the law really is.

We can't be saved by obeying the law, and God never intended that we could. The purpose of the law is not to save us. The purpose of the law is to identify sin and show us our need of a Savior. Paul compares the law to a tutor who leads us along to Jesus so that we can be saved by faith in His righteousness (see Galatians 3:19–25).

The apostle James illustrates the same idea with a mirror. Just as a mirror shows us what our faces truly look like, the law shows us what our spiritual conditions really look like: "But be doers of the word, and not hearers only, deceiving yourselves. For if anyone is a hearer of the word and not a doer, he is like a man observing his natural face in a mirror; for he observes himself, goes away, and immediately forgets what kind of man he was. But he who looks into the perfect law of liberty and continues in it, and is not a forgetful hearer but a doer of the work, this one will be blessed in what he does" (James 1:22–25).

When I go to Mount Sinai and look at the Ten Commandments God gave there, it makes me realize how much I need a Savior. The law makes me realize my need. I might get the idea that I'm OK until I hold the law up against my life and see how short I fall every day. It is like a mirror.

Every once in a while, I go out and get on my

tractor to clear some trees and burn branches on my land. I am out there working and sweating and wiping my brow. I don't always realize how dirty I am. But when I stop working and go inside, hot and sweaty, and look in the mirror, I can see all the dirt and grime and sweat.

What does the mirror tell me? It tells me that I need to clean up. I don't take the mirror off the wall and try to wash my face with it, though. The mirror can't make me clean; it just tells me that I need to get clean.

James says that's how it is with God's law. The law shows me how unclean I am spiritually. It tells me I need to wash in the blood of Jesus. His blood, His righteousness, is the only thing that can wash away my sins. The law cannot save me; that's not its purpose. Its purpose is to show me how much I need the Savior. It's designed to lead me to Jesus. I am saved only by grace, by His righteousness. But does that mean the law is done away with? Does that mean that saved Christians don't need to keep God's law? Not at all.

Satan's *fake news* says that God's law has been abolished this side of the Cross, but the apostle Paul emphatically disagrees. "Do we then make void the law through faith?" he asks. "Certainly not! On the contrary, we establish the law" (Romans 3:31). Could anything be clearer than that?

"But," someone says, "Paul specifically says that the law was nailed to Christ's cross. Doesn't that mean that Christians aren't subject to the law—it doesn't apply now?"

Let's see exactly what Paul says. Jesus "wiped out the handwriting of requirements [KJV: "ordinances"] that was against us, which was contrary to us. And He has taken it out of the way, having nailed it to the cross" (Colossians 2:14). In another place, Paul speaks of Christ "having abolished in His flesh the enmity, that is, the law of commandments contained in ordinances" (Ephesians 2:15). What is he talking about? The Ten Commandments? No, he is talking about "the law of commandments contained in ordinances."

Before Jesus came to Earth to live and die for us, God gave His people an object lesson of the plan of salvation. That object lesson was the sanctuary, with its offerings and festivals and ceremonies and sacrifices and rituals and symbols. There were ordinances covering all these things. These pointed forward to Jesus, the Lamb of God who would come to take away the sins of the world (see John 1:29). The Bible calls these ordinances "a shadow of things to come" (Colossians 2:17). They served their purpose until Jesus came.

Then the symbols that pointed forward were swallowed up in the reality of Jesus' great sacrifice. Animal sacrifices and ceremonies of cleansing were no longer needed because the real sacrifice had already been made by Jesus at the cross. That's why the veil in the temple was torn from top to bottom at the moment of Jesus' death (Matthew 27:51). Those commandments of ordinances were nailed to Jesus' cross. We don't have to sacrifice a lamb today because our Savior already died for us. Look at the Ten Commandments. Do you see any sacrifices mentioned there? Any offerings? Any ceremonial cleansings? Any religious rituals?

God's Ten-Commandment law is eternal. Jesus said it will last as long as heaven and the earth remain.

If Satan's *fake news* can't deceive you into believing that God's law has been abolished, then he'll try to get you to believe the *fake news* that you have to keep God's law in order to be saved. Once you accept that, he'll try to lead you down one of two paths: He'll try to get you to become a legalist—someone who tries as hard as possible to keep God's law in his own strength by building up his willpower and worrying that he has somehow failed in some tiny, insignificant matter. Failing that, Satan will try to convince you that keeping God's law is a great burden and a crushing load to carry—so great that you might as well not even try. And so you give up and forget about obeying God at all. Satan doesn't care what aspect of his *fake news* you accept, as long as he can lead you away from God.

Let me make something as clear as I possibly can. No one is saved by keeping the law—even God's great Ten-Commandment law. We are saved by grace alone through the precious blood of Jesus. But the same Savior who died for us says, "If you love Me, keep My commandments" (John 14:15). Don't you think that people saved by the blood of Jesus would *want* to keep the commandments that the Savior has given? Of course, they would! Not in order to *be* saved, but because they *have been* saved.

We keep the commandments because we love Jesus, because we want to please Him, and because He asks us to. The apostle John says, "Now by this we know that we know Him [Jesus], if we keep His commandments" (1 John 2:3).

Motive makes all the difference. Paul says, "He who loves . . . has fulfilled the law. . . . Love is the fulfillment of the law" (Romans 13:8, 10). We show our love for God by keeping His commandments. We don't keep them to be saved. And when we keep the commandments from the motive of love, we will find that Jesus was right when He said, "For My yoke is easy and My burden is light" (Matthew 11:30). John writes, "For this is the love of God, that we keep His commandments. And His commandments are not burdensome" (1 John 5:3). The psalmist testified, "I delight to do Your will, O my God, and Your law is within my heart" (Psalm 40:8).

That is what God wants to do for you. He wants to put His law in your heart. He says, "This is the covenant that I will make with them after those days, says the LORD: I will put My laws into their hearts, and in their minds I will write them" (Hebrews 10:16). When God's law is in your heart, it is easy to obey. When God's law is in your heart, you will want to do what He commands because you love Him. God so loved us that He gave His only Son (see John 3:16). Jesus so loved us that He left heaven to live on Earth and die in our place. We respond to that love by loving and obeying Him. "Love is the fulfillment of the law" (Romans 13:10).

---

1. Rachel E. Morgan and Grace Kena, "Criminal Victimization, 2016," Bureau of Justice Statistics, December 2017, https://www.bjs.gov/content/pub/pdf/cv16.pdf.

2. Federal Bureau of Investigation, "Table 17: Percentage of Offenses Cleared by Arrest of Exceptional Means," *Crime in the United States,* 2016, https://ucr.fbi.gov/crime-in-the-u.s/2016 /crime-in-the-u.s.-2016/tables/table-17.

3. "Percentage of Births to Unmarried Mothers by State," 2016, Centers for Disease Control and Prevention, https:// www.cdc.gov/nchs/pressroom/sosmap/unmarried/unmarried .htm.

CHAPTER 6

God's Special Day

Fake News

1. The Sabbath is part of the Old Testament law that was done away with at the cross when Jesus died.

2. This side of the Cross, the Sabbath has been changed from the seventh day of the week (Saturday) to the first day of the week (Sunday), which Christians should keep in honor of the day Jesus rose from the dead.

My wife, Camille, and I spent the summer before my senior year in college high up on Idaho's Sourdough Peak in the Nez Perce National Forest in a fire lookout cabin. We watched for signs of forest fires and worked on college credits by correspondence. It was a great summer! Eventually, we had to leave, and we headed east in our Volkswagen (VW) Bug, back to college in Michigan. We drove at night because it was cooler.

A VW Bug doesn't use a lot of gasoline, but it does require filling up once in a while. Somewhere between Des Moines and Chicago, I noticed the gas gauge showing I needed fuel. I stopped at a gas station and filled up, then got back on the highway heading east toward Chicago. At least that's what I thought. Unbeknownst to me or to Camille, I had gotten turned around and was driving back toward Des Moines, which we had driven through a couple of hours earlier.

It was nighttime, and I didn't see any highway signs to alert me to my mistake. Besides, I have an excellent sense of direction—most of the time. Camille will tell you, though, that if I get turned around, I'm really lost. After driving about seventy miles, I spotted a bus and noticed that the sign on the front said "Chicago." *That bus driver must have forgotten to change his sign*, I thought. It had still not dawned on me that I was driving west. Even when I'm turned around, I'm confident that I'm going the right way; I just knew that I was right and the bus driver was wrong.

I eventually realized my mistake. There was only one thing to do: turn around.

I'd *thought* I was driving east toward Chicago. I'd *thought* I was nearing my destination with every mile. But the reality was very different, and I ended up driving an extra 150 miles that night.

A person may sincerely think he's right and still be sincerely wrong. That's true when he's driving at night on the highway, and it's also true spiritually. The Bible says, "There is a way that seems right to a man, but its end is the way of death" (Proverbs 14:12).

On a typical Sunday, the fast-food restaurants in your town—Taco Bell, Wendy's, McDonald's, Subway, and so on—are open for business and crowded with customers. But not Chik-fil-A. The late S. Truett Cathy, the founder of Chik-fil-A, closed his stores on Sunday, and his family still does. Hobby Lobby does the same. The owners of these companies sincerely believe that Sunday is the Lord's sacred day and that it should be kept holy. They back up their beliefs with action.

I think it's fantastic when Christians stand up for what they believe to be right, but I also believe it's important to make sure that the truth they're standing up to support is really true. Like the owners of Chik-fil-A and Hobby Lobby, many sincere Christians believe that the seventh-day Sabbath, which God instituted at Creation, has been changed to Sunday and that we should now worship on the first day of the week.

There's just one problem. Nowhere in the Bible does it tell us to keep Sunday holy. Nowhere does the Bible say that God's seventh-day Sabbath has been changed. Satan has been hugely successful in convincing the majority of Christians that the Sabbath has been changed from Saturday to Sunday.

When was it changed? Who changed it? By what authority? Where in God's Word do we find a record of the change? If God had changed His day of worship, don't you think He would have pointed that out in the Bible?

Have you ever wondered why there's so much

confusion about which day is God's holy day? Why is one group of sincere Christians—the majority—worshiping on Sunday, while at the same time, a smaller but equally sincere group of Christians worships on Saturday? It's clear that Satan's *fake news* is at work here. Both groups are sincere, but both groups can't be right. Remember that it's possible to be sincere—and be sincerely wrong.

"Does it really matter?" someone asks. "Isn't one day as good as another? After all, you're still worshiping God whether you worship on Saturday or Sunday."

Maybe so. Maybe it doesn't matter—unless it matters to God. If it's just a question of one day or another, it doesn't really matter. But if it's a question of "the truth that is in Jesus," that makes a difference, doesn't it (Ephesians 4:21, NIV)? If the Bible makes it clear that Jesus is intimately connected to His Sabbath—if the Bible makes it clear that it's a matter of following Jesus and His truth—then it's no longer just a question of days. Then it matters, because it matters to our Savior.

What does the Bible say about Jesus and the seventh-day Sabbath?

When Jesus was here on Earth with us as a human being, He declared that He was "Lord . . . of the Sabbath" (Matthew 12:8). What did He mean, and how is Jesus the Lord of the Sabbath?

First of all, Jesus is Lord of the Sabbath because He instituted the Sabbath Himself at Creation. Jesus is the Creator. The Bible says, "By Him [Jesus] all things were created that are in heaven and that are on earth. . . . All things were created through Him" (Colossians 1:16). So when Genesis describes Creation, we need to remember that Jesus Himself is the Creator. Here's how the Bible describes the origin of the Sabbath at the end of Creation week: "On the seventh day God ended His work which He had done, and He rested on the seventh day from all His work which He had done. Then God blessed the seventh day and sanctified it, because in it He rested from all His work which God had created and made" (Genesis 2:2, 3).

Our Redeemer is also our Creator. He gives us eternal life by His death, and He gave us physical life by His creative power. That's why the Bible tells us that the seventh-day Sabbath is a sign of His redeeming, sanctifying power in our lives (Ezekiel 20:12, 20).

God placed the seventh-day Sabbath in the very heart of His Ten-Commandment law and pointed to Creation as the reason for weekly rest and worship on His special day. The fourth commandment says: "Remember the Sabbath day, to keep it holy. Six days you shall labor and do all your work, but the seventh day is the Sabbath of the LORD your God. . . . For in six days the LORD made the heavens and the earth, the sea, and all that is in them, and rested the seventh day. Therefore the LORD blessed the Sabbath day and hallowed it" (Exodus 20:8–11).

Could God be any clearer? He tells us here which

day is His holy Sabbath—the seventh day of the week. He tells us how and why we are to keep it. We can search the Bible from cover to cover without finding any other day that God has asked us to keep holy. In fact, we can't really keep a day holy that God has not made holy.

Why, then, do so many sincere Christians believe Satan's *fake news* that the seventh-day Sabbath has been changed to the first day, Sunday?

One reason some people give for the change is that they see the seventh-day Sabbath as the Jewish Sabbath. They believe that it was given to the Jews, but that Christians should keep Sunday in honor of the day Jesus rose from the dead.

Is that true? Did God make the seventh-day Sabbath only for the Jews? Remember that God instituted the Sabbath at Creation. Were there any Jews at Creation? Were Adam and Eve Jewish? Were they Irish or German or French? Obviously not. Adam and Eve were of no nationality; they were just human beings. Nationalities and races of humans did not appear for centuries after Creation. God didn't make the Sabbath for the Jews because there weren't any Jews at Creation. He gave the seventh-day Sabbath to all humanity at Creation.

Another reason some people give for believing that the Sabbath was changed from the seventh day of the week to the first is that Jesus' resurrection took place on Sunday. "We keep Sunday in honor of the Resurrection," they say.

But the Bible says nothing about commemorating

the Resurrection by worshiping on Sunday. A little later in this chapter, we'll look at the New Testament texts mentioning the first day of the week in connection with the Resurrection, and we'll see that they say nothing about honoring that day.

Some people believe that keeping the seventh-day Sabbath is a legalistic attempt to earn salvation—that Sabbath keepers are legalists. Why should keeping the fourth commandment be any more legalistic than keeping the eighth (do not steal), the seventh (do not commit adultery), or any of the other nine commandments? A person *might* be keeping the Sabbath in a legalistic attempt to earn salvation. That person might also avoid stealing or killing or committing adultery for the same legalistic reason.

Sabbath keeping, from the right motive, is not legalism any more than obedience to any of the other commandments is. We don't keep the Sabbath *in order* to be saved. We keep it because we *have been* saved. There's a big difference.

Finally, many Christians believe that God's law, including the seventh-day Sabbath, was done away with at the Cross and that Christians are under grace, not law. In the previous chapter, we saw the biblical truth that we can't save ourselves by keeping the law. We are saved only by grace through our faith in Jesus' great sacrifice on the cross. But this doesn't mean that God's law is not important. It doesn't mean that once we have been saved by faith in Jesus' blood, we are free to disregard His commandments.

As the apostle Paul put it: "A man is justified by faith apart from the deeds of the law. . . . Do we then make void the law through faith? Certainly not! On the contrary, we establish the law" (Romans 3:28, 31).

Suppose you're driving down the highway one morning, late for work, and all at once you see flashing red-and-blue lights behind you. You look down at your speedometer and see that you're driving twenty miles per hour over the speed limit. Suppose the police officer comes up and asks for your license and registration, and then the officer hands them back and says, "You know you were speeding, but I'm not going to give you a ticket. I'm just going to give you a warning."

You deserved a ticket, but the officer forgave you. Would that make it all right for you to get back out on the highway and start driving twenty miles per hour over the speed limit again? You were saved from a ticket by the officer's grace, but the law still applies to you. In fact, it applies all the more because you were forgiven. That's the way it is with God's law as well. Keeping the seventh-day Sabbath is not legalism. It's showing your love by being obedient to the One who has saved you by His grace.

Why, then, do the majority of Christians today accept Satan's *fake news* that God's holy day—the seventh-day Sabbath—has been changed to Sunday, the first day of the week? We have seen that the Creator set aside the seventh day at Creation by resting on it, blessing it, and making it holy. We have seen that He has commanded us to keep it holy.

Is there anything in the New Testament that would lead us to believe there has been a change? Does God want us to keep Sunday now that Jesus has died on the cross? Let's look at every text in the New Testament that mentions the first day of the week. There are only eight.

The first six texts all refer to the same event—Jesus' resurrection:

1. Now after the Sabbath, as the first day of the week began to dawn, Mary Magdalene and the other Mary came to see the tomb (Matthew 28:1).

2. Now when the Sabbath was past, Mary Magdalene, Mary the mother of James, and Salome brought spices, that they might come and anoint Him [Jesus]. Very early in the morning, on the first day of the week, they came to the tomb when the sun had risen (Mark 16:1, 2).

3. Now when He [Jesus] rose early on the first day of the week, He appeared first to Mary Magdalene, out of whom He had cast seven demons (verse 9).

4. Now on the first day of the week, very early in the morning, they [women from Galilee], and certain other women with them, came to the tomb bringing the spices which they had

prepared (Luke 24:1).

5. Now the first day of the week Mary Magdalene went to the tomb early, while it was still
   dark, and saw that the stone had been taken
   away from the tomb (John 20:1).

6. Then, the same day at evening, being the
   first day of the week, when the doors were
   shut where the disciples were assembled, for
   fear of the Jews, Jesus came and stood in the
   midst, and said to them, "Peace be with you"
   (verse 19).

Each of the Gospel writers agrees that Jesus rose
from the dead early on Sunday morning and that
Mary Magdalene and other women came to the
tomb to anoint His body with spices. The writers
say nothing about changing Sabbath to Sunday and
nothing about Jesus' followers honoring His resurrection by worshiping on the day He rose from the
dead.

Some have thought that the last of these six
verses, John 20:19, is describing a worship service
on Sunday evening that the disciples held in honor
of their risen Lord, but this wasn't a worship service. John says the disciples were there with "the
doors . . . shut . . . for fear of the Jews." They were
huddled together, afraid that the Jewish religious
leaders who had killed their Master would come
looking for them. In fact, Mark and Luke make it
clear that the disciples didn't even believe Jesus was
alive that Sunday evening, until He appeared to

them (Mark 16:9–11; Luke 24:9–12, 36–44).

These six texts give no evidence of a change of the Sabbath to Sunday. Let's look at the last two texts that mention the first day of the week.

Acts 20:7, 11 says, "Now on the first day of the week, when the disciples came together to break bread, Paul, ready to depart the next day, spoke to them and continued his message until midnight. . . . When he [Paul] . . . had broken bread and eaten, and talked a long while, even till daybreak, he departed."

This was clearly a religious meeting held by the apostle Paul on the first day of the week. Does this mean that the seventh-day Sabbath was changed and that now Sunday is God's holy day of worship? Let's look more closely.

First, this is the only known instance when the apostles held a religious service on the first day of the week. If you read the entire chapter of Acts 20, it seems clear that this was a special farewell meeting. Paul had been at Troas for a week, and he held this night meeting because he was "ready to depart the next day" (verse 7).

Second, Paul's regular worship custom was to observe the seventh-day Sabbath (Acts 13:14, 44; 17:2; 18:4).

Third, Acts 20:7, 11 says nothing about the Sabbath being changed and doesn't tell Christians to now begin worshiping on Sunday.

Fourth, holding a religious service on a particular day doesn't make that day holy or establish a practice—especially since God has specifically designated the seventh day as His Sabbath. Many churches hold a midweek service on Wednesday evening, but that doesn't make Wednesday holy or make it into the Sabbath.

Fifth, Acts 20:7 says that the disciples "came together to break bread" on this special night meeting. Some have seen special significance in this fact, but Acts 2:42, 46 says that the early Christians got together *daily* to break bread and pray.

Acts 20:7, 11 is probably the strongest New Testament text for those who believe the Sabbath has been changed. When we look at the context, though, we see that it says nothing about such a change.

The final text in the New Testament mentioning the first day of the week is 1 Corinthians 16:1–3. The apostle Paul is writing to the Christians in Corinth about a collection of money he was taking up in the churches for the Christians in Jerusalem. He tells them: "Now concerning the collection for the saints, as I have given orders to the churches of Galatia, so you must do also: On the first day of the week let each one of you lay something aside, storing up as he may prosper, that there be no collections when I come. And when I come, whomever you approve by your letters I will send to bear your gift to Jerusalem."

Some have said that this text indicates a weekly meeting on Sunday in which offerings were collected. But Paul's instructions make it clear that this is not a public collection. Paul tells them to "lay something aside" at the beginning of each week and store it up until he comes. The text mentions no church service at all.

We have now looked at every text in the New Testament that mentions the first day of the week—all eight of them. We've seen that they give no hint of a change in God's holy day. In spite of Satan's *fake news,* the Bible is clear that the seventh-day is still God's Sabbath. It is the day Christians this side of the Cross should keep holy.

Another text we'll look at doesn't mention the first day of the week, but it does speak of the Lord's Day—a title that's often applied to Sunday. The apostle John says in Revelation 1:10, "I was in the Spirit on the Lord's Day."

In other words, John received visions from the Holy Spirit on a day he calls "the Lord's Day." He doesn't say which day of the week that was. Is there any way to know which day is the Lord's Day? Yes, there is. Jesus said, "The Son of Man is Lord even of the Sabbath" (Matthew 12:8). If any day can rightfully be called the Lord's Day, it must be the day of which Jesus Himself claims to be Lord.

As we have seen, the Bible doesn't speak of a change of God's Sabbath from the seventh day of the week to the first. God didn't change it. He included the Sabbath in the heart of His Ten Commandments. And He says, "My covenant I will not break, nor alter the word that has gone out of My lips" (Psalm 89:34). He also says, "For I am the

LORD, I do not change" (Malachi 3:6).

Jesus didn't change the Sabbath. He kept the seventh-day Sabbath while He was here on Earth (Luke 4:16). He said He was Lord of the Sabbath (Matthew 12:8). He said the law would stand as long as there is heaven and earth (Matthew 5:18; Luke 16:17). He said, "If you love Me, keep My commandments" (John 14:15).

The apostles didn't change it. As we have seen from their writings, they give no sign that any such change has taken place since Jesus' death and resurrection. The apostle Paul habitually worshiped on the seventh-day Sabbath (Acts 13:14, 42; 16:13; 17:2; 18:4). He testified, "For I have not shunned to declare to you the whole counsel of God" (Acts 20:27). But he said nothing about changing the Sabbath.

How, then, did the change take place?

Paul further declared, "For I know this, that after my departure savage wolves will come in among you, not sparing the flock. Also from among yourselves men will rise up, speaking perverse things" (verses 29, 30). That is exactly what happened. After the apostles died, many errors quickly came into the early church—including observing Sunday as the Sabbath. It was all part of Satan's plan to introduce *fake news* into the church. His *fake news* about God's Sabbath is still at work in the church today.

Some time ago I was holding evangelistic meetings in a church in Houston, Texas. The name *Gilley* is fairly well known around Houston because country singer (and my distant cousin) Mickey Gilley got his start there. A lot of people attended my meetings because my name is Gilley, and some of those people were interesting, to say the least!

One night I had just starting preaching when I heard a mighty roar outside the church. A motorcycle club was riding into the parking lot. They got off their Harleys and came into the church—leather jackets, bandannas, and all. They sat together.

They listened to the sermon, and they came back the next night and the next and the next. I soon saw that they were genuinely interested in knowing what the Bible said about the topics we were studying. One night John, the leader of the motorcycle club, came up front after the meeting to visit with me. He said that the club members had pretty rough backgrounds, but they had come to Jesus and left their old lives behind. They were now a Christian motorcycle club. "We're looking for a name for our club," John told me.

I suggested the name *Sons of Thunder*. That's the nickname Jesus gave to His disciples James and John (Mark 3:17).

The guys liked that name. A few nights later they showed up in their new black leather jackets with "Sons of Thunder" across the back in red. They kept coming to the meetings night after night, studying what God had to say in the Bible and accepting the truths they were learning. They rejected Satan's *fake news.*

One night during the meetings, I preached

about the truth of God's seventh-day Sabbath. We looked at the same texts we've been looking at in this chapter. John accepted the Sabbath truth and so did several other members of the club. But others rejected it strongly and argued with John.

One of his friends said, "John, don't you know that God doesn't care which day you keep?"

"If that's true," John replied, "then He won't mind if I keep the day He told me to keep in His Bible, will He?"

That was a great reply. You can never go wrong following God.

The real question is this: Will we obey God, or will we obey man? Will we follow a man-made tradition, or will we obey God's Sabbath commandment? Will we believe Satan's *fake news* or God's truth as it's taught in His Word? The Bible says of God's people in the days just before Jesus returns, "Here is the patience of the saints; here are those who keep the commandments of God and the faith of Jesus" (Revelation 14:12).

Don't you want to be one of the saints following Jesus and obeying His commandments? I know I do. I want to keep the day Jesus made holy at Creation. I want to keep the day Jesus kept while He was here on Earth. I want to keep the day Paul kept. I want to show my love for my Savior by obeying Him and worshiping Him on His holy Sabbath day.

CHAPTER 7

Knowing and Following Truth

In this book, we've been looking at the devil's *fake news* versus God's truth. The devil says, "Here are some alternative facts. Truth isn't all important."

What about it? Is truth really important? It is to God—so much so that Jesus came to this earth to live and to die on the cross for it.

Is it important to you and me? We all say yes, but do we really mean it? We look back through history at martyrs who were burned alive at the stake for the truth as it is in Jesus, and we say, "I, too, would have given my life for Jesus."

Would we? If we're afraid to live for Him today, would we have given our lives for Him then? How likely is it that we would have had the courage to die for Him back then if we're afraid to stand up to friends, family, and society today and proclaim, "I won't follow the *fake news* that Satan has planted. No matter what, I will follow the Bible and the Bible only as my guide." If we're unwilling to follow what God says regardless of what the majority is doing now, would we have been martyrs for the truth then? If we won't follow the truths of His Word in times of ease today, would we have done so in times of persecution? You and I know the answer.

When Jesus was accused by the Jews, Pontius Pilate asked Him,

> "Are You a king then?"
>
> Jesus answered, "You say rightly that I am a king. For this cause I was born, and for this cause I have come into the world, that I should bear witness to the truth. Everyone who is of the truth hears My voice."
>
> Pilate said to Him, "What is truth?" (John 18:37, 38).

Because of the compromises he had made in his life, Pilate was no longer able to hear the voice of conscience, which Jesus says is His voice. When we turn our backs on the clear truths of God's Word, we'll come to a place of such confusion that, like Pilate, we cannot discern truth.

Today Jesus is not asking us to literally die for the truth; He's asking us to be determined to live for Him, which always means dying to self and putting on Christ. So what do I do about the devil's *fake news* that seems to have entered into the teachings of most churches? How do I hear and respond to Jesus' voice of truth?

I do this by clinging to the Word of God and letting it be its own interpreter. I do so by not basing a belief on one or two isolated texts that seem to say the exact opposite of what the rest of the Bible clearly indicates. What the Bible says—that's the important thing. In the Bible, we find the truth as it is in Jesus. Jesus says, "I am the way, the truth, and the life" (John 14:6). You can never go wrong in following Jesus, His Word, and His example.

"Oh, but no one is saved by his own effort," someone says, "and we are certainly not saved by keeping the law."

This is "true and also correct," as a friend of mine used to say to emphasize that something was a fact. In Matthew 5, Jesus magnifies the law and shows us that it's not enough just to refrain from adultery, but that lust itself is sinful. It's not enough to refrain from killing our neighbor—even hating him is a sin.

So as Jesus emphasizes the far-reaching aspects of His law, we begin to see that our only hope is in Him, not in obedience to the law. Just because we can't be sinless in our own strength, though, doesn't mean that we go around killing, stealing, and committing adultery. Of course not!

Someone may chime in, "But that's the last six commandments Jesus is talking about—not the first four."

Does that mean that the first four are done away with? That you can have another god, make graven images, or take God's name in vain? That you can forget that God is the Creator? Why does Satan create so much *fake news* about the Sabbath, which is enshrined in the heart of God's Ten Commandments?

Every November I take a group of people to Israel

on a Bible enrichment tour. At sundown on Friday, we go to the Western Wall in Jerusalem to watch the Jewish people—especially the Hasidic Jews, who are ultraorthodox and much like the Pharisees of old—welcome the Sabbath. It's a beautiful thing, and you would be blessed in going there with us.

When the Jewish people leave the wall, though, they walk home because they can't drive a car on the Sabbath. They must also live nearby because they can only walk a Sabbath day's journey. When they get home, they can't turn on a light switch or start a fire—and on and on with 667 of the same kinds of laws that Jesus, when He was here, clearly pointed out as man-made rules that make the Sabbath a burden. Those burdensome rules are an extreme that Satan loves because they not only tie up people in legalism but also turn off everyone else who sees them.

Jesus was sinless. He never broke the Sabbath. He wrote the Ten Commandments with His own finger and He knew that these man-made Sabbath rules were not His law. He never meant for the Sabbath to be a burden; He meant it to be a wonderful day of rest, worship, and renewal—truly a blessing that everyone should benefit from, not the burdensome curse that the religious leaders had made of it.

If the devil can't get us to fall into that legalistic ditch, then he has another *fake news* story. He tells people, especially preachers, that the Sabbath has been done away with and that they can "forget" the day God said to remember. They don't always get this story straight, giving many different rationales for abandoning the seventh-day Sabbath.

Some say that God has changed His mind about the Sabbath and has decided we should now worship on Sunday—in spite of the fact that God says He does not change (Malachi 3:6). They can't prove it from Scripture, and of course, we have the historical record that Roman emperor Constantine took it upon himself to introduce Sunday worship in A.D. 321. History is clear on this, so the Christian church must not have been keeping Sunday before A.D. 321. Otherwise, why would Constantine decree a change? He wouldn't have made the change and decreed something Christians were already doing, would he?

Historians, especially those who study church history at seminaries, know this. Most pastors who have studied church history know the truth but hide behind a twisting of Paul's writings. But the Bible is clear that Paul *didn't* teach that the Sabbath was done away with. On the contrary, numerous Bible texts point out that Paul not only kept the Sabbath but warned against lawlessness, which is breaking any of God's commandments. Yet Satan's *fake-news* campaign on this point has been very successful.

A number of years ago I became acquainted with a minister licensed by a very large church in the Dallas–Fort Worth area. We worked on some projects together, which involved meeting with the governor of Texas, the vice president of the United States, and a number of senators. This pastor was actively involved in the temperance ministry.

One day he asked me why I kept the Sabbath. I studied the Bible with him on the subject. He continued with his study and soon was completely convinced that Saturday, the seventh day, was the Sabbath and was still binding upon each of us.

He then went to the senior pastor of the church where he was licensed—a famous pastor who was known around the world—and told him of what he had learned in the Bible about the Sabbath. The senior pastor agreed with him and said that he had known this for many years. In fact, he said that he himself kept the Sabbath from sundown Friday until sundown Saturday just as the Bible indicates we should.

My friend was amazed and asked him why he didn't share that truth with the congregation. The senior pastor said that if he told his congregation this truth on Sunday morning, he would no longer be the pastor of that church by Sunday night. The board of deacons would fire him, he said. Tradition is so strong that few have the courage to follow God's Word.

This same senior pastor had a secretary who lived next door to a friend of mine who was a member of a Sabbath keeping church. One day, as this secretary was visiting with my friend and his wife, the secretary told them that her boss believed in the Sabbath just as they did. She said she asked him, "Why don't you join their church?" He never gave an answer.

I could tell you of many more such instances. Through a common love of Honda Gold Wing motorcycles, another friend of mine became friends with a well-known televangelist. This TV pastor asked my friend why he kept the Sabbath. My friend offered to have his own father, who was a retired pastor, study with the televangelist. This his father did, and the televangelist was convicted of the truth about God's holy day. He called another friend who was also teaching on TV and shared his newfound truth. This friend said, "I've known that for years; but if you teach that on the air, you'll lose your financial support and you won't be on the air in six months." Like the rich young ruler, the televangelist walked away.

Have you ever noticed how all the politicians of a given political party will provide the same answer to some question that comes up? They're given talking points that often twist the truth or put a certain spin on a topic. Many pastors, while in seminary, are given talking points to answer the question of why they keep Sunday when there is no biblical reason and history clearly shows when and how it was changed. In time, they actually believe these talking points. The devil continues to trip up even good, sincere people with the biggest lie he's ever told against God and His law. But thank God that more than twenty million people in one Christian fellowship around the world have said, "We will follow God and keep His Sabbath holy."

"But I'm in good company by keeping Sunday,"

someone says. "The great majority of Christians worship on Sunday."

That is true. Ministers of Protestant churches, priests of the Catholic Church, and all the popes do, along with millions of the faithful. But does that make it right? Is truth determined by a popular vote? Making that which is right appear wrong is a specialty of the devil and his *fake news.*

While driving to the airport in St. Louis recently, I saw a billboard advertising the services of a criminal attorney. The sign said, "Just because you did the crime doesn't mean you are guilty!" In other words, this attorney was saying, "Hire me, and I will twist the truth so cleverly that I can confuse twelve jurors into thinking that you are innocent." That is exactly what the devil has done with his *fake news.*

Let's look at the other group—those who keep the seventh-day Sabbath. This group includes all the Bible writers from Genesis to Revelation; all the apostles, including Paul; all the early Christians, both Jews and Gentiles; and there, standing head and shoulders above everyone, is Jesus—who, according to the Bible, not only kept the Sabbath but gave us the Sabbath. He is the great "Lawgiver, who is able to save" (James 4:12). That's a pretty good group to belong to.

Remember the answer that John, the leader of the Christian motorcycle club, gave to those who told him God didn't care what day he kept? "Well then," he responded, "He won't mind if I keep the day He told me to keep." God has told us to keep only one day holy—Saturday, the Sabbath.

Let's say that I keep the seventh-day Sabbath. In the day of judgment, Christ, our High Priest and our Judge, asks me, "Jim, why did you keep the Sabbath?"

I answer, "Because You gave it to us at Creation, before there was sin and thousands of years before there was a Jew. You gave it again on Sinai, writing it with Your own finger in the heart of the Ten Commandments. All the Bible writers kept it. You kept it when You were here on this earth, and You told us that those who are waiting for You when You come will be a commandment-keeping people."

But what if, instead, I decide to follow the crowd and keep Sunday? Judgment Day comes, and Jesus looks at me and says, "Jim, why didn't you keep the Sabbath when I clearly told you in My Word that you should?"

What can I say? That I didn't believe it was important? That I didn't think He cared what day I kept? That everybody else was keeping another day other than the Sabbath? That Dr. So-and-So said it didn't matter or that it had been changed? None of those answers would hold up in the day of judgment, would they?

In that day, I'm sure that you, like me, want to hear Jesus say, "Well done, good and faithful servant; you were faithful over a few things. . . . Enter into the joy of your lord" (Matthew 25:21).

Truth—God's truth—is important. If you would like to dig deeper into the topics we've looked at in